Teach Me to Love

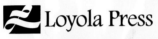
Loyola Press

There were once two children
who wanted to love God
and their neighbors,
but they did not know how to love.

The two children went to the girl who lived
next door.
"Please teach us to love," the children said.
But the girl cried and said, "I'm too sad."

So the little boy said,
"Come with us, and we'll cheer you up."
And the sad girl felt much better.

The two children and the sad girl
went to the boy across the street.
"Please teach us to love," the children said.
But the boy shook his head and said,
"I'm too hungry."

So the little girl said,

"You can share my lunch."

And the hungry boy felt much better.

The two children
and the sad girl
and the hungry boy
went to the girl down the road.
"Please teach us to love," the children said.
But the girl scowled and said,
"I'm too angry."

So the little boy said,
"I'll listen to what you say."
And the angry girl felt much better.

The two children
and the sad girl and the hungry boy
and the angry girl
went to the twins around the corner.
"Please teach us to love," the children said.
But the twins laughed and said,
"We're too naughty."

So the little girl said,
"I'll forgive you."
And the naughty twins felt much better.

The two children and the sad girl
and the hungry boy and the angry girl
and the naughty twins went to the boy across
the vacant lot.
"Please teach us to love," the children said.
But the boy sighed and said,
"I'm too lonely."

So all the children said together,
"Come with us and be our friend!"
And the lonely boy felt much better.

Then the lonely boy and the naughty twins
and the angry girl and the hungry boy
and the sad girl went home with the two
children who wanted to learn how to love.

Their father and mother were very happy
to see all the children, and they had a party.

That evening at bedtime,
the two children said to their parents,
"Please teach us to love."

Their mother hugged them both and said,
"You have cheered your sad friend
and fed your hungry friend."
Their father gave them each a kiss and said,
"You have listened to your angry friend,
forgiven your naughty friend,
and shared with your lonely friend."

"It's easy to love our friends,"
the little boy said.
"But how do we love God?"
"Is God our friend?"
the little girl asked.

"God is our friend," their father said.

"God cheers us when we are sad.

God feeds us when we are hungry."

"God loves us," their mother added.

"God listens to us when we are angry.

God forgives us when we are naughty.

And God shares with us when we are lonely."

As the children went to sleep,
the little boy said,
"I love God and Mommy and Daddy and
all our neighbors."

"And," the little girl added,
"God and Mommy and Daddy and all our
neighbors love us."

"Thank you, God, for loving us
and for teaching us how to love."

Loyola Press

3441 North Ashland Avenue
Chicago, Illinois 60657

©1999 John Hunt Publishing; Text ©1999 Pennie Kidd
Illustrations ©1999 Toni Goffe

Design by Graham Whiteman

ISBN 0-8294-1369-3

Printed in Hong Kong/China

99 00 01 02 03 / 10 9 8 7 6 5 4 3 2 1